DATE DUE

AUG 1 3 2015	

DEMCO, INC. 38-2931

©2010 by Design Media Publishing Limited
This edition published in May 2011

Design Media Publishing Limited
20/F Manulife Tower
169 Electric Rd, North Point
Hong Kong
Tel: 00852-28672587
Fax: 00852-25050411
E-mail: Kevinchoy@designmediahk.com
www.designmediahk.com

Editing: Yeal Xie
Proofreading: Maggie Wang
Design/Layout: Hai Chi

ISBN 978-988-19739-8-6

Printed in China

Lobby & Lounge

Edited by Yeal Xie

DESIGN MEDIA PUBLISHING LIMITED

Contents

Almyra Hotel

Cyprus

The hotel has undergone an ultra-chic metamorphosis and now features sleek interior elegance inspired from the island's patron goddess of love and beauty, Aphrodite.

Splashes of the 1970s' boldness – such as white leather sofas and ottomans – are enhanced by a combination of natural and artificial lighting. Seeing as the hotel places as much emphasis on a successful family experience as on good design, the concept focuses on the practical as well.

1. The warmly-lit cosy ottomans
2. The skylight brings in natural lighting
3. The giant pendant lamp in a simple shape
4. Picturesque view outside the window
5. The combination of natural and artificial lighting

Aloft

Montreal, Canada

A design concept set to raise the bar in affordable select-service hospitality, offering airy, bright loft-like guestrooms, enhanced technology services, landscaped outdoor spaces for socialising day and night, and an energetic lounge scene. Envisioning a series of urban oasis on the American roadside, Rockwell has emphasised sophistication, community, functionality, and comfort.

The experience encourages guests to spend more time out of their rooms – the exterior, lobby, guestrooms, bathrooms, and backyard, pool area and corridors all serve as public gathering spaces. Special features and visually distinctive iconic structures capture the visitor's eyes, including a carport, an abstract roof-line and colourful glowing linear light sources on the exterior – design inspired by the notion of travel landscape and motion.

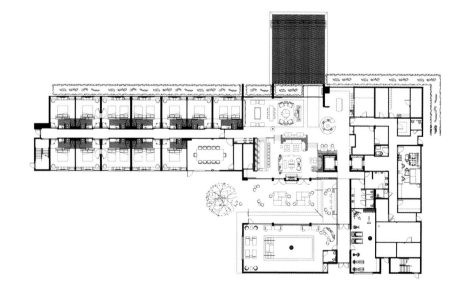

1. Sitting area in the lobby
2. Modern lobby
3. Bar counter at one side of the lobby

Ames Hotel

Boston, USA

The new Ames Hotel is a boutique hotel that occupies the historic Ames Building. Although the design for the all-new interior of the space paid homage to the original 19th century exterior, Rockwell Group provided a modern framework for the lobby. Original elements were re-interpreted to complement the elegant and innovative new design.

The lobby features an original marble mosaic tile vaulted ceiling, a dramatic marble and brass staircase. Scattered around the lobby are original site-specific art works such as a chandelier of thousands of reflective discs suspended over the floor on wires, and an abstract ceramic wall installation behind the reception area made up of many pieces of hand-cast porcelain.

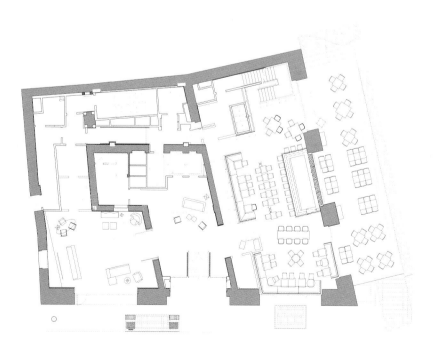

1. The bright colour becomes the focal point of the neutral-palette space
2. View of the lobby
3. The sumptuous chandelier

Andel's Berlin

Berlin, Germany

The hotel revitalised a former apartment building by Studio Aldo Rossi near Alexanderplatz. This unfinished concrete structure has been abandoned shortly after the Berlin Wall came down and remained empty ever since.

The concept is built off the solid foundation of the Andel's brand principles. Function and comfort are given equal priority, to accommodate the needs of both business and leisure guests. The spaces are uncluttered and crisp but softened by focused textural enhancement. Materials are carefully chosen to be discrete but effective. Colours are to be fun and stimulating but also calming. Above all, the design is understated but memorable.

1. Sofa providing a good rest
2. Reception
3. Panorama of the lobby

Andel's Lodz

Lodz, Poland

Three stacks of elliptical light wells are punched through the full height of the building. These tapes are aligned obliquely, perceived as unified cones, reaching up through five floors to a glazed rooflight. These "light cones" create a holistic experience on the ground floor and on every bedroom floor, unlocking an ever-changing combination of framed views up to the sky and down to the animation of the lobby and lobby bar. Daylight is channelled to illuminate the heart of the deep, open-plan ground floor lobby bar, and by night, coloured light stains the ellipses to create towering, kinetic sculptures, or films are projected onto them to create distorted, abstract cinemas, adding discrete animation to the calm space.

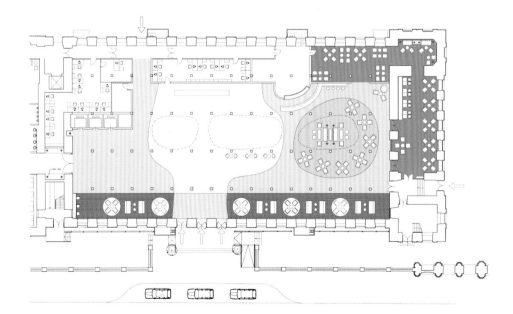

1. Special chairs
2. Oval opening for light
3. The open lounge
4. The reception counter
5. A romantic atmosphere is achieved through lighting

BALANCE holiday HOTEL

Zell am See, Austria

Its inviting understated modern design not only generates an atmosphere of relaxing elegance, but is sensitively implemented to promote inner balance. The holistic concept behind the BALANCE holiday HOTEL aims to create a sense of "flowing privacy", a homogenous space that always places the individual at the centre.

The curve lobby feels natural and warm. Several simple potted plants are adopted so that the space is clear but not monotonous. On one side of the lobby is the sitting area where the shelves are adopted as interior partitions. In this way, the designers created a series of semi-private areas. The shelf partitions are quite practical; further more, they would not interfere with the openness of the entire space.

1. Leisure area
2. Lobby

Busan Paradise Hotel

Busan, Korea

The overall concept of the Busan Paradise Hotel is modern classic. It has some of the elements of traditional classic spaces with a modern GAIA touch. The lobby which has a traditional colonnade that leads into an open height vertical area with sunken seating living rooms and oversize modern/classic chandeliers above every seating area. With the hotel's geometry "grid", the space flows tranquilly into each other. Every niche and space has its own character. The lobby entrance acts as a contemporary art gallery. Bright materials, smooth surfaces and luxurious stone flooring were selected for this area. The lighting is mostly indirect, creating a soft, warm ambience.

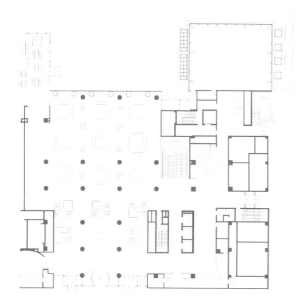

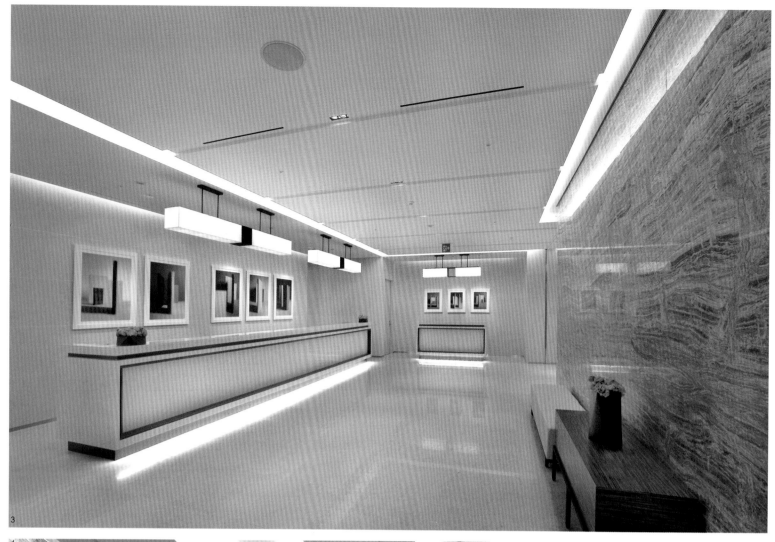

1. The pattern on the floor continues to the wall
2. The columns and the sofas are well-lined
3. The simple and clear interior design
4. The colour green extends throughout the hotel
5. Unique floor pattern

Ca' Sagredo Hotel

Venice, Italy

In the golden and precious Music Ballroom, numerous frescoes attributed to Gaspare Diziani completely cover the walls and ceiling.

Splendid chandeliers in gold leaf hang from the ceiling, and the floor is embellished with the coat of arms of the Sagredo family. The frescos on one wall act as a camouflage for a door to the secret passage which once led to the "Casino Sagredoz".

The staircase was just a part of an overall renovation projected for the palace. Two marble cherubs by Francesco Bertos decorate the entrance to the staircase, glancing to the incoming guests. The floor is in mosaic, decorated with elegant coloured volutes.

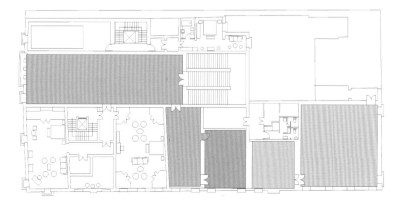

1. Frescoes in the ballroom
2. Frescoes near the staircase
3. Detail
4. The classic interior and the elegant staircase
5. The arch
6. A glimpse of the ballroom

Camino Real Hotel Monterrey

Monterrey, Nuevo León, Mexico

The architectural concept is set out to take advantage, in the best way, of the views and sunlight. In the inside, there is a lobby of four levels, giving presence and solemnity to the reception area.

Red is chosen to be the colour palette of the lobby, aiming at a home-like warm atmosphere. A series of comfortable cloth sofas were arranged in the lobby so that guests could have a relaxing rest. Lighting design is a key for the designers. Soft lights diffuse from the ceiling, walls and the floor. The square holes on the thick walls are a repetitive element. The inner surfaces of the holes are painted red, creating a variable and warm environment when natural light comes in.

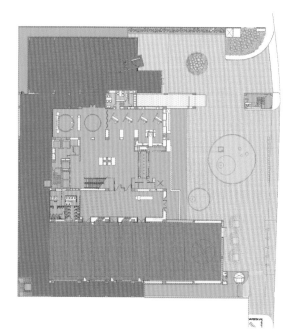

1. The lounge
2. Natural light comes in from the holes
3. The red-palette interior
4. The lounge
5. Lighting creates a warm atmosphere
6. The entry hall
7. View of the entry hall from the floor above

Central Palace Una Hotel

Catania, Italy

A prestigious building dating back to the early 1900s, in the artistic and commercial heart of Catania, was already an historical luxury hotel. The restoration project has been carried out in the view of maintaining the Sicilian style and traditional cultural heritage.

The hall represents symbolically the indoor of a Mediterranean palace's sunny courtyard. The restaurant of the first floor is partially covered with long curtains and, with the lounge of ground-floor and big stairs, it gives onto the hall. The floor is done by cobblestone paving of lava stone embellished by a decoration of white Siracusa stone which recalls the courtyards of historic buildings in old baroque style and awards to the area a central value.

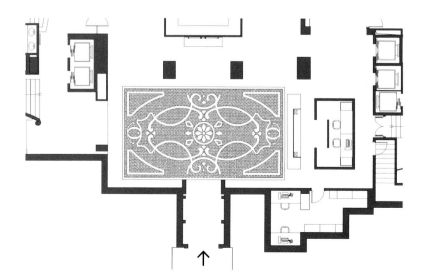

1. View of the lobby from the entrance
2. Distinctive floor decoration
3. Lounge
4. A corner of the lobby
5. Entrance

Chiswick Moran Hotel

London, UK

Housed in a 1960's former office building, the concept for the hotel is "West Coast/West London". The vibe is a contemporary evocation of the 1960's California, a link between this happening area of London and the glamour of LA.

A palette of heavily veined marble and stained oak boarding unites a flowing sequence of lobby, bar and restaurant. Above the double height lobby is a vast bespoke polished steel and plexi-glass chandelier. There's no complicated decoration in the lobby except the sumptuous chandelier. The surfaces of the wall and the floor are all designed simple and orderly. The use of geometric patterns typically represents the style of modernism and simplicity.

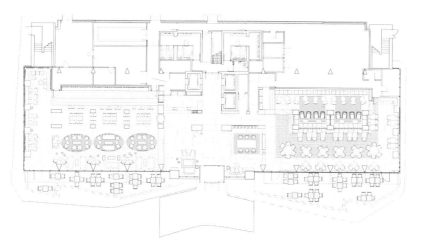

1. The simplicity-styled lobby
2. View of the dining area from the lobby

Crowne Plaza Hotel, Changi Airport

Singapore

The architecture and interior expression is derived from Southeast Asian textiles and tropical jungle. The façade is a three-dimensional batik fabric that provides 60% shading to the façade. Naturally ventilated and lit corridors are lined with a warp of horizontal painted bands against the weft of coloured vertical aluminium panels. The public areas are wrapped in flowing bands of timber veneer, glazed Thai tiles, Indonesian batik and Chinese metal mesh. The ballroom is an abstracted forest under a ceiling of raintree canopies in perforated metal. Materials are intentionally rough, sensuous and intense, contrasting in colour, texture and solidity to counteract the blandness of commercial aviation environment.

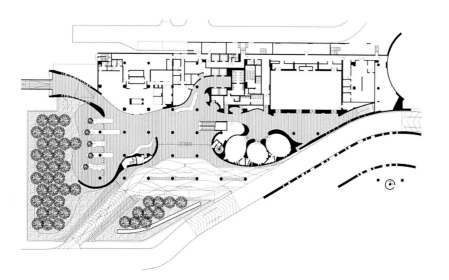

3

1. With the "branches" on the walls, the "soil" on the floor, and the "sunshine" on the ceiling, on entering the hotel, guests would feel as if stepping into a rain forest
2. The green carpet brings in some natural air
3. Aerial view of the lobby overflowing with vigour
4. Plants are used as decoration, creating a natural green space

Epic Hotel & Residences

Miami, USA

Down-lighting highlights chiseled limestone walls and figurative bronze sculptures, while rhythmic slats in a dark walnut finish create a backdrop for Epic's lobby lounge. Italian-inspired modular sofas and sleek lounge chairs create inviting conversation areas under glowing amber glass chandeliers.

Epic's guests are greeted with a white onyx reception desk resting under a monolithic frame in a pearl cream Venetian plaster finish. The four-tiered silver mica chandelier by Neidhardt cascades a warm glow over camel-coloured leather feature chairs and an amorphic-patterned wool area rug.

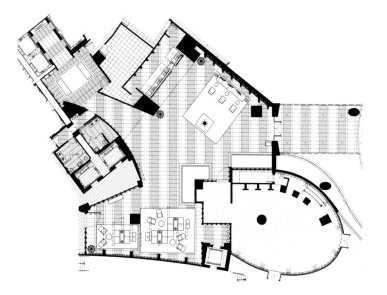

1. Sitting area in the lobby
2. White onyx reception desk

Fitzwilliam Hotel

Belfast, Ireland

The designers have referenced some traditional domestic typologies, the inglenook in the lobby being the most significant of these, in which they have created a cosy fireside, timber-panelled and book-lined nook nestling beneath the glass box of the private dining room. Yet within this setting the furnishings are edgy: white leather sofas on a black and gold carpet to their bespoke design, using a deco-inspired motif based around the letter "F". A game of contrast is deliberately played – the drama of the double height lobby against the intimacy of the inglenook, the luxurious book-matched Levanto marble of the reception desk against the quarry tiled floor, white lacquered tables against black and white shag pile rugs.

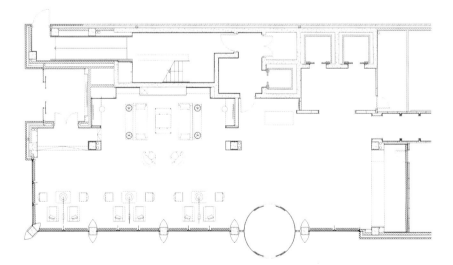

1. The lounge is arranged around the fire place
2. The reception
3. Brilliant interior lighting
4. Aerial view of the lobby with eye-catching lamps

Four Seasons Hotel Firenze

Florence, Italy

Four Seasons Hotel Firenze is a living museum of art history, set within the walled tranquility of Florence's largest private garden. The Hotel comprises two Renaissance palaces. Today, the Hotel's colourful history unfolds through its ornately painted and crafted interiors, which have returned to their original beauty following seven years of painstaking restoration.

The designers restored the old time luxury and elegance with fabrics, furnishings, etc. The narrow area along the window is arranged as a lounge. Warm sunshine casts in through the curtains hung on the ceiling on the sofas wrapped in red fabrics. Here guests could enjoy the afternoon leisure once privileged to the nobility.

1. The lounge immersed in sunshine
2. The symmetrical sofas and decoration in classical style

Fresh Hotel

Athens, Greece

The Fresh boldly mixes rich natural materials, such as oak and walnut wood, with bright pink and orange, making it a clean-lined sanctuary from the flurry of downtown Athens just outside its doors. A generous fireplace that is surrounded by an imposing black wall stands opposite the reception created by an attractive pink glass box.

Between the bar counter and the fireplace, several sofas and coffee tables in peculiar shapes are arranged, completing a relaxing space and at the same time serving as a kind of decoration for the lobby. The overall design of the lobby is simple and clear, where guests would feel relaxed as soon as they step in.

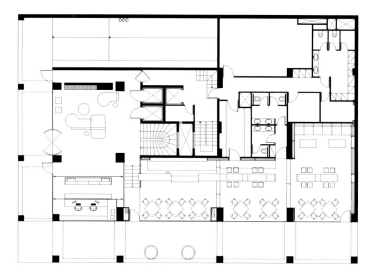

1. The pink glass reception
2. The double-height black wall with the fireplace

Gerbermühle Hotel

Frankfurt, Germany

Primarily built as a flour mill in the 1520s, the Gerbermühle is, however, better known as the summer residence of J. Wolfgang von Goethe and his beloved Marianne von Willemer. Since the beginning of the 21st century, it has earned a reputation as popular tavern and place of excursion.

The interior design creates a warm ambience reminiscent of a traditional guesthouse, harmoniously combined with modern furniture and excessive light. The generous and vast garden on the bank of the River Main offers comfortable seating in the shade of beautiful, old trees, an ideal haven where business men meet excursionists and families meet friends.

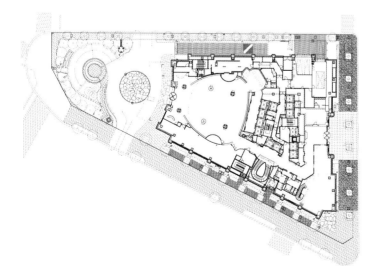

1. Warmly-lit lobby
2. Lobby

Golden Sands Resort by Shangri-La, Penang

Penang, Malaysia

Golden Sands Resort by Shangri-La, located on Penang's popular Batu Feringgi beach, is a veritable tropical paradise for vacationers and families.

Cool Lounge, the resort's newest addition, pampers guests with the comforts of home and acts as a transit lounge for early arrivals and late departures. It is designed with an emphasis on space and comfort, and the open-air concept allows guests an expansive view of clear blue sky and sea blending in harmony with the lush tropical greenery. The lounge, as with the main lobby area, is decked out with vibrant red and green plush cushions, and features creamy wooden carvings of kelp designs symbolic of the ocean.

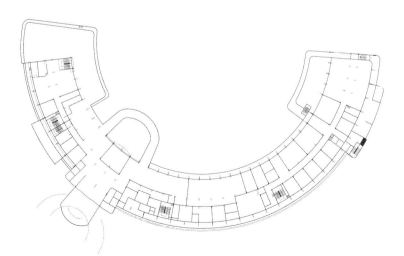

1. Interior view of Cool Lounge
2. Interior view of Cool Lounge
3. Exterior view of Cool Lounge

Haymarket Hotel

London, UK

A bold step away from cookie-cutter minimalism, Haymarket Hotel fuses contemporary and classical references in an ultra-central London location. A landmark building designed by the legendary John Nash.

The façade features a dramatic row of columns that run the length of Suffolk Place. Interiors are a remarkable combination that honours the building's noble lineage while updating it with co-owner Kit Kemp's "modern English" interpretation of interior design. The lobby is a clean airy space featuring a large stainless steel sculpture by Tony Cragg and paintings by John Virtue.

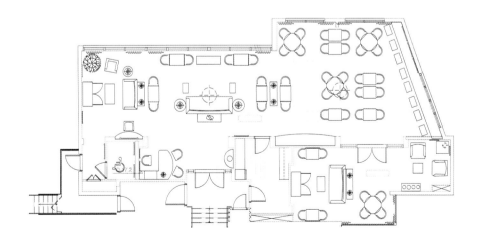

3

1. The artistic sitting area
2. The marble-like pattern feels cool and noble
3. A corner of the lobby
4. Lobby reception
5. The yellow colour offers the feeling of the sun

Hospes Madrid

Madrid, Spain

Originally an affluent apartment house with wrought-iron balconies designed in 1883 by architect José María de Aguilar, the handsome red brick Hospes Madrid is an icon of Bourbon Restoration period architecture. So the Hospes Design Team needed to take special care that their modern additions were in harmony with the building's historic elements. This gracious sense of hospitality extends throughout the hotel, where a tranquil, opulent ambience is achieved through white marble and gold details offset by dark fine wood.

Guests eager to experience the landmark in its original glory will be relieved that despite a dominant minimalist style, the original mouldings, columns, wrought iron and woodwork remain intact.

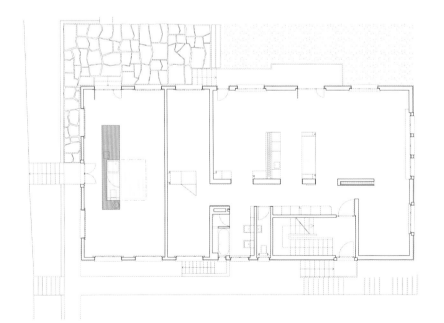

1. A corner of the lobby
2. The sitting area is also a good place to work
3. Sitting area in the court
4. Sitting area

Hotel ALL'ALBA

Padua, Italy

Located in one of the most prestigious areas of Abano Terme, a considerable place for thermal baths, Hotel ALL'ALBA is just a few kilometres away from Padua, Venice and Verona. Hotel ALL'ALBA has been terminated in 2008 after only three years of work (2005 – 2008).

Hotel ALL'ALBA is characterised by the strong sensibility of its classic forms established by the wise use of precious materials, the marble flooring of its hall of reception at the entrance, the halls for the holidays and the refined restaurant. The spaces of the halls are extremely refined in every detail, from the flooring to the decoration on the wall and on the ceiling, the colour of the curtain and the solution for the furniture in a unique style.

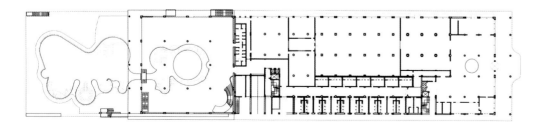

1. Classical styles are incorporated in every detail of the interior design of the lobby
2. Piano music would improve the noble classic environment

Hotel EOS

Lecce, Italy

The Eos Hotel, named after the Greek goddess of the dawn, is the beginning of a new concept in hotels, a concentration of tradition and cutting-edge, a pilot structure that shies away from the traditional notion of hôtellerie by proposing fifteen different types of rooms, united by a design in close harmony with the architecture, the colours, the materials and the distinctive features of Salento.

The spacious lobby features the French windows on both sides, through which both the path leading to the entrance of the hotel and the quiet backyard can be seen. The reception in the lobby is particularly designed, with a balance established between function and styling. For example, the peculiarly-shaped seats in the corner are very eye-catching, as a turning point leading to the restaurant.

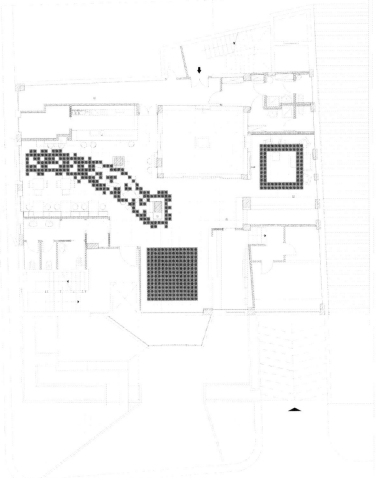

1. Detail of the reception
2. Decorative elements of the floor
3. Reception
4. Spacious and open lobby

Hotel Mod05

Verona, Italy

Hotels have two souls: a public one, which presents the dynamic of the arriving and departing zones, brings the idea of encounter, activity and leisure; and an intimate and protected one, designed for the night and the rest. The Hotel Mod05 is the overlap of two buildings, divided without touching each other by a large stripe of glass. The compact but light volume of the rooms floats above the complex and articulated ground floor.

The ground floor builds itself around a glassy central space which brings together different functions: the reception, the office, the bar, the restaurant, the meeting room and the kitchen. The strength of the volumes is highlighted by the treatment of the surface, the continuity of the finishing and the contrast of colours between the interior and the exterior.

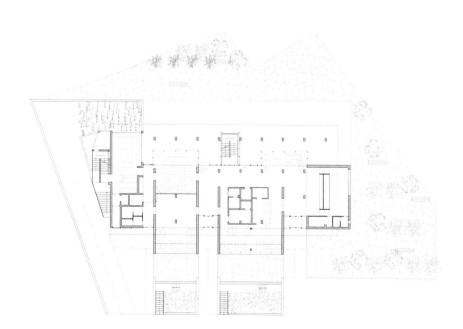

1. Entrance
2. Counter in the middle of the lobby
3. Reception and sitting area
4. Sitting area
5. The architectural structure determines the peculiar space

4

5

Hotel Modera

Portland, USA

The Hotel Modera is a complete renovation – transforming a neglected motor lodge, often thought of as an eyesore, into one of Portland's sleekest places to stay. The new design restores the simple lines of the 1964 building and pays homage to the mid-century origins.

The new lobby's floor-to-ceiling glass connects the courtyard and integrates the indoors with the exterior. Walnut flooring that wraps to the walls, together with Calcutta marble and rich fabrics, melts the simplicity of the architecture with warm tones and inviting textures – allowing sculptural furnishings and provocative artwork to steal the show.

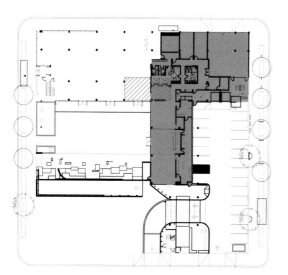

1. Overall lobby
2. A corner of the sitting area

Hotel Monaco Alexandria

Alexandria, Virginia, USA

The traditional wood-panelled walls are painted a vibrant "Naples Blue" – emulating the strong tonal colours of early colonial interiors. The ebony chevron-patterned wood floor offers a sharp contrast to the bold walls and completes the saturated architectural backdrop for this eclectic space. The Monaco signature "trunk" design of the registration desk is given a twist by way of cardinal red leather covering and exquisite nailhead detailing. Just behind the desk stand meticulously stenciled panels covered in an arabesque pattern. An oval dome in the lobby's ceiling provides a natural focal point and is punctuated by a dynamic chandelier composed of multicoloured glass and silk orbs.

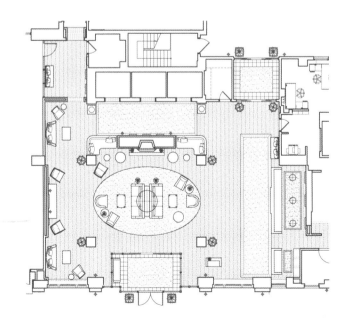

1. Unique interior décor
2. The lounge

Hotel Murano

Tacoma, Washington, USA

Given the commission to renovate this weathered chain hotel, the design team looked to the flourishing local art community for influence.

Taking the hotel lobby back to its original, pure architecture offered a harmonious environment for art glass installations. It was critical that the backdrop be minimal and neutral to allow the art to be the focus. Art glass is incorporated into the architecture – the front desk, entry doors, lobby chandelier and public restroom sinks were all created by internationally known artists. A cool blue glow floods the entrance and lobby bar through stacked glass walls while the bar itself has a slump glass counter, illuminated from within.

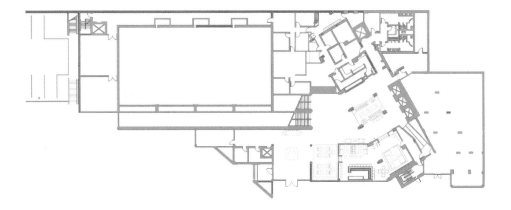

1. Sitting area in front of the counter
2. Brightly-coloured bar counter
3. Sitting area beside the fireplace
4. Overlook at the lobby

Hotel Palomar Arlington

Arlington, Virginia, USA

Taking inspiration from the hotel's very location – a striking glass and steel tower rising from the banks of a historic river, the design team created the sophisticated, inviting interiors of this four-star hotel based on contrast and balance – earth and water, modern and traditional, feminine and masculine.

The characteristic Palomar fireplace – this time clad in slabs of honey onyx – stands as a sentinel, providing light, warmth and intimacy in separate conversation groupings. With a nod to a traditional Men's club, the high-backed wing chairs mix with more feminine, curvilinear sofas and rounded ottomans. Taupe and chocolate brown fabrics combine with flourishes of magenta just as a tailored suit might be accented by a beautiful silk tie.

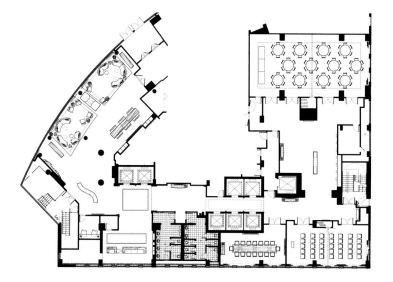

1. The reception
2. A corner of the lounge
3. Decoration at the end of the corridor
4. The cosy lounge
5. Detail of the reception counter

Hotel Palomar Dallas

Dallas, USA

The unique structure of the hotel was originally conceived by the acclaimed architect Ralph Kelman in the 1960s. The new hotel was designed to capture this prosperous Dallas momentum and create a sense of place that is distinctly Dallas.

Passing through the entry vestibule, the guest's gaze sweeps upward. Rectilinear planes in variable sizes, heights and painted ivory values execute a dynamic ceiling detail. This motif is reiterated in the flooring. Large wood floor fields of alternating value and scale create contrast and depth.

Contributing to the hotel's sense of place and echoing its architecture is the extensive art programme, inspired by the artist and sculptor, Donald Judd.

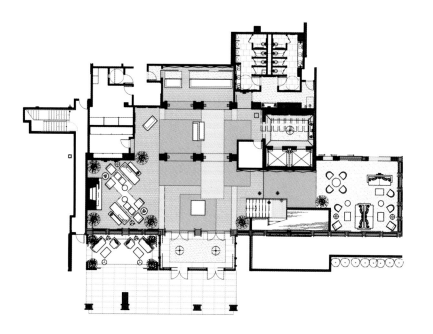

3

1. Rectilinear planes in variable sizes, heights and painted ivory values execute a dynamic ceiling detail
2. Illuminated decorative glass fills vertically-oriented openings to catch attention day and night
3. Cylindrical amber glass candles suspend gracefully above a cantilevered stair
4. The simplicity, geometry and repetition relayed in Judd's work are demonstrated in the inherent lines of the hotel's architecture
5. Geometry and purity of form were points of departure in developing a dynamic, contemporary, sophisticated mix of abstraction, texture, realism, colour accents, lightness and darkness

Hotel Palomar Los Angeles

Los Angeles, USA

Aging and dilapidated, with low ceilings and a cramped, dark lobby, this Doubletree Hotel was an out-of-place eyesore in desperate need of a complete renovation.

Guests enter on a wenge and white oak chevron-patterned wood floor that creates a dramatic exclamation point under chocolate custom carpets with carved cream-coloured tropical leaves. In the lobby, warm platinum walls envelop the space, a soft palette to host the richness of macassar ebony and wenge millwork. An overscaled decorative bronze mirror running the length of the lobby reflects the stunning ceiling-height rouge marble fireplace. The shimmer of suspended acrylic panels serves as a dramatic backdrop for inviting curved sectional seating.

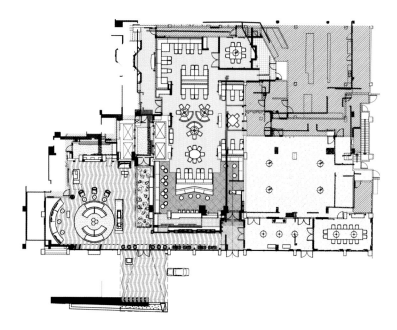

1. Back-lit patterned glass panels lead guests to the macassar ebony and platinum leaf registration desk
2. The hues of taupe, chocolate and French grey come alive with accents of crimson, aubergine and hints of silver
3. Wenge and white oak chevron-patterned wood floor
4. Sumptuous textiles elegantly cover deco-inspired furniture shapes
5. Touches of glass and polished chrome add sparkle and energy to the interiors and dramatic red lacquer walls, reminiscent of the lips of Hollywood sweethearts, draw guests into the lift lobby and up to the guestrooms above

Hotel Palomar Washington

Washington D.C., USA

Hotel Palomar features an interior that boasts tailored architectural elements with the use of exotic woods, high contrast, refined furnishings and inspiring bold artwork. The result is an inviting visionary and serene environment for an aesthetically sensitive international traveller.

Passing through the entry doors, flanked by the grand two-storey entrance, a guest is welcomed by full-height architectural panels. Bathed in light, these two opposing waterfall-inspired decorative walls are sculpted and then finished in a lustrous patina. Italian Murano glass chandeliers with cream-coloured tones draw the eye through the space to a striking feature wall adorned with sleek ebonised wood panelling pierced by glowing white onyx stone blocks.

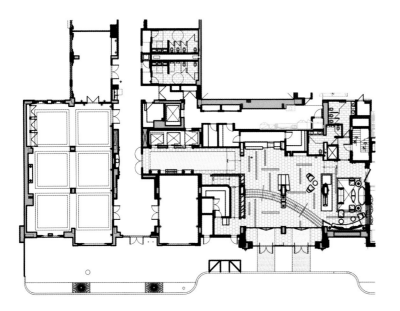

1. A warm glow emanates from a full-height architectural light element, leading the guest to registration

2. The woolen rug from Nepal in the lounge is a unique feature

3. The lounge

4. A corner of the lobby

5. The furnishings in the lobby are chic and novel

Hotel Rho Fiera Milano

Milan, Italy

A sober and functional building dating back to the early 1900s has been transformed into a contemporary business hotel as the result of an important operation in industrial archeology. Where cotton was once woven, now new business relationships will be woven.

The top floor boasts a convention room, fitness and wellness area; the first floor has a reading room decorated with white lacquered boiserie, while the lobby features an eye-catching red, studded leather reception desk. The common denominator of the space is a dramatic lamp that spans the entire structure and the completely renovated wrought-iron floral balustrade that runs the length of all the floors.

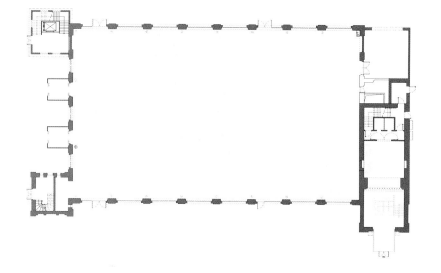

1. The front-facing windows have been naturally kept and play a key role in lighting the rooms
2. The flood of light beams casts an enchanting play of light and shadow

Hotel Ritter

Frankfurt, Germany

At the reception and in the lobby area, coloured accents welcome the guests. The highlights here are the cuckoo clocks – typical German clocks from the black forest – not adopted in the traditional way. The usual world times are displayed by accentuating white cuckoo clocks on a fuchsia coloured wall. To deal sensitively with the charm and the tradition, the interior designers reacted with a certain sense of humour.

In the lobby, some different kinds of lounge furniture are arranged, all in brown cream tones, fitting well in this historical building. The eye-catcher here is the pink-coloured sofa with its floral pattern – bringing grandma's times to mind. This sofa is newly combined with the wall of fame of this hotel.

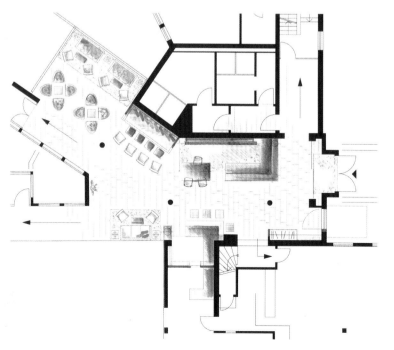

1. The fuchsia wall is decorated with the clocks
2. The pink sofa in the lobby is eye-catching
3. Detail of the clocks

Hotel Villa & Resort Luisa

San Felice del Benaco, Italy

The restyling relates to the duality between the existing territory and the sober modernity, readable both inside and outside the structure. This dualism has resulted in the work through a continuous curved line that links the interior design with the outdoor area, boosted by exchange of materials and finishes, a particular lighting design and a sophisticated use of ceiling plaster.

Neutral colours and natural materials of the tradition are a tribute to the local culture; the "circle" and shades of white were thought to highlight the contemporary style of the structure. An important use of transparencies and reflections is the bridge between design and folklore.

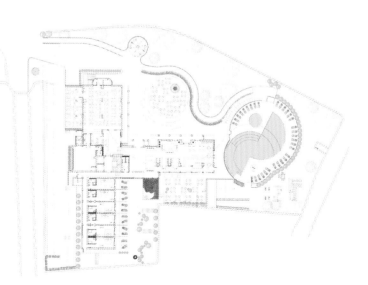

1. The reception
2. The continuous white ceiling plaster is used throughout the public spaces in the hotel

Hotel Watt 13

Milan, Italy

In the building which recalls the long art history of Milan, the designers decided to use light as the key element after a thorough consideration about the architectural characteristics and available technologies. The careful choices of furniture and furnishings enhanced the simple and clear hotel interior. In the 700-square-metre lobby, the skylight and the horizontal windows spread on the walls bring in sufficient natural light. The designers didn't interfere with the interior too much. The open spaces are defined by the arrangement of furnishings. The furnishings are all in black and white, with simple yet stylish shapes. As the key element, the lamps display their uniqueness and simplicity. Sometimes they are hid in the construction of the building, and the diffusion of light helps create the desired ambience.

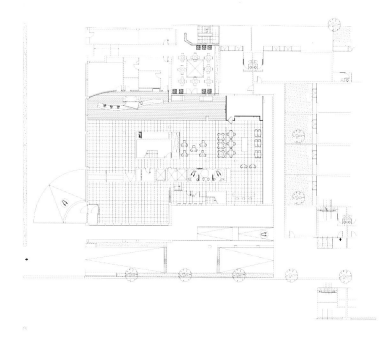

5

1. At the bottom of the reception, golden lighting diffuses out
2. Peculiar-shaped sofas are arranged beside the windows
3. The open spaces flow into each other
4. The black sofas define a small lounge
5. Spot lighting in the corridor

Ink 48

New York, USA

The hotel lobby is a luxurious interpretation of a pocket park – the small and sometimes hidden urban parks that animate New York's streets – exhibited in rich textures and surfaces. Upholstered panels with large-scale graphic floral patterning flow continuously from wall to ceiling. Green bamboo marble floors and walnut wood surfaces contrast with the robust exposed concrete columns of the lobby and textured stone tile walls. Open wooden screens embrace the custom-designed seating furniture pieces in the living room area, providing a private and relaxing territory for guests. The immersive red colour of the cabanas creates intimate tucked-away environments within the lobby. Across from the cabanas is the lobby bar with an onyx bar top, and a back wall made of stacked vertical slats leaving room for the bottles of liquor illuminated from behind and above.

1. The lobby with the seating area
2. The reception
3. In the lounge, artistic decorations are adopted on the seats and the wall

InterContinental Hotel

Abu Dhabi, UAE

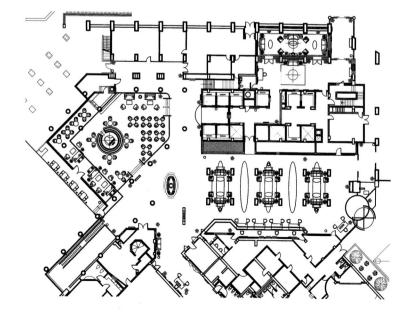

The sleek, clean, contemporary architecture of the existing building's exterior is the inspiration for the interior design approach to the hotel. As guests enter the main lobby, they walk across polished warm grey granite floors punctuated with polished black granite striping accentuating the width of the space. Centralised seating groupings with contemporary glass waving light fixtures above are flanked by a procession of stainless steel-clad columns leading to a textured glass water feature. The opposing walls of the main lobby space are clad in a warm honey onyx, simply detailed and back-lit.

At reception, a simple curved wall of glass with cascading water forms a backdrop to the desk and continues the same welcoming, cooling experience as the lobby.

1. The lobby with an unusual depth
2. Detail of the reception
3. Symmetry and sumptuous décor endow the hotel with an air of nobility
4. The reception

I-Point Hotel

Bologna, Italy

I-point Hotel has been designed for business people, very dynamic, and always on the move, that normally will spend a very short time, normally a couple of nights per stay. Hence the choice of orange and red colours as symbol of energy, is combined with wood finishing, to deliver a different and new, but warm and delightful atmosphere.

The lobby is designed with the dynamism of a modern metropolis. The designers carefully selected a series of furniture, which livens up the lobby atmosphere with simple look and bright colours. Such a style continues for the interior decorations in the lobby. Besides, many potted plants are adopted as interior scenery, bringing the air of nature into the lobby.

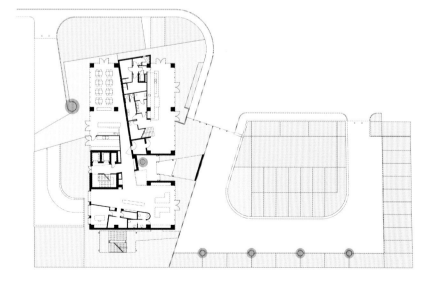

1. Sitting area in the lobby
2. Seats on the balcony
3. Efficient use of every space to offer good rests

JinxiuJingya Hotel

Beijing, China

Here is a cosy and tranquil underwater world. Looking upward, you could see ripples overlap on the ceiling and fishes swim leisurely around you. Or, in the quiet sea you could feel the sunshine cast in which seems to allure you to step into a mysterious world. The JinxiuJingya Hotel is such a place which impresses you with the underwater experience.

The front entrance with overwhelming golden finishes and the arc patterns on the ceiling create an environment reminiscent of the play of light and shadow underwater. Lounge areas are arranged in the overall open space, providing both spacious and private spaces.

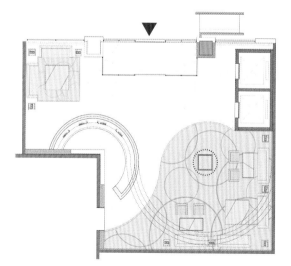

1. The entrance to the lobby from which guests step into a mysterious underwater world
2. Guests could find a tranquil underwater world with the unique subdividing of space
3. The decorative curves and lighting all bring an underwater experience to guests

JW Marriott Hotel Beijing

Beijing, China

Located in the central district, the contemporary hotel anchors China's central place. Upon check-in at one of the five individual reception desks, guests can move into the rectangular-shaped lobby lounge.

The entire lobby is immersed in a warm yellow colour palette. The space is decorated with forms and lines rather than complex colours. The spiral stair meanders from the ground floor to the first floor, completing the spacious double-height lobby. The interior landscape in the centre of the lobby, the platform at the foot of the spiral stair, the columns in the interior and the décor on the ceiling are all well integrated into the space, which is a great piece of art itself.

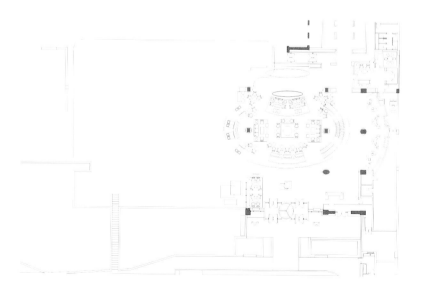

1. The spiral stair
2. The elegant curves surround the lobby

Kempinski Pragelato Village & Spa Piedmont

Turin, Italy

The inspiration for the project began with the Medieval Town of Pragelato and the smaller village of Plan which neighboured the resort, and was to become the home for the duration of the project. The deisgners studied the local architectural vernacular, and were infused with the local history. They were greatly inspired by the local materials, and decided to use them to design in more modern forms.

Wood, stone, glass, wrought iron, wool, cashmere and other natural and sustainable materials all feature strongly in the interiors for the hotel. The designers studied the colours of other mountain regions throughout the world and let these inspire their choice for fabrics, wall and floor finishes and the furniture design.

1. The white reception desk becomes the focal point in the dark-palette lobby
2. A glimpse of the lobby with the glittering white reception
3. The open lounge where stone brings a natural air
4. The unsophisticated furnishings

KLAUS K

Helsinki, Finland

Klaus K is set in a national romantic-era building, at the top of the Esplanade on the tree-lined street Bulevardi. Helsinki airport is less than 20km from the hotel. Inspired by the emotional contrasts of Finland's national epic, its nature and drama, the hotel bears the stamp of Finland's finest architectural and literary traditions.

The Klaus Kurki hotel, a landmark for many years, has been transformed into the Klaus K with the help of renowned Finnish architects SARC Group and international interior design by Stylt Trampoli. The Klaus K aspires to go further and "take the hotel out of the hotels": creating an ultra-designed lifestyle experience where contrasts abound, such as the Renaissance-inspired space of the Rake Sali ballroom and the playfully-designed theme rooms and suites – the hotel delivers a luxurious experience of tradition and cutting-edge Nordic modernity.

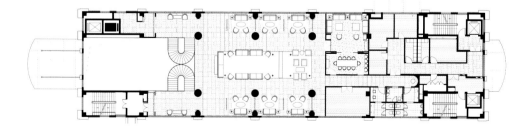

1. Romantic and comfortable environment in modern style
2. The reception counter
3. Careful details: magazines are prepared in the lounge
4. Lighting, furniture and fabrics contribute to the home-like warmth

Kruisheren Hotel

Maastricht, The Netherlands

Located in the picturesque Kommelplein Square in central Maastricht, the Kruisheren Hotel is a remarkable conversion of a Gothic church and monastery, a tour de force synthesising the original 15th-century architecture and dressed-down modernism. The spectacular arches of the church, dating from 1438, now cover the integrated reception area, which also offers conference rooms, a library, boutique and coffee bar.

An outstanding feature is the newly-installed mezzanine where guests are served breakfast while taking in views of Maastricht through the chancel windows.

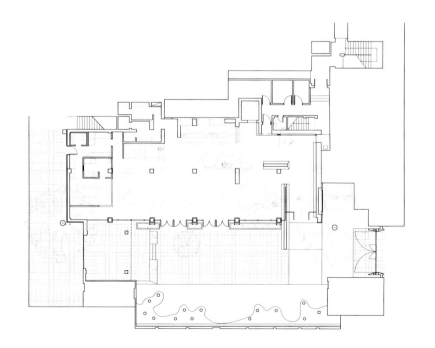

1. The decoration on the wall is reminiscent of the monastery
2. Exquisite decoration on the vault
3. Aerial view of the lounge
4. History and modernity is integrated in the lounge
5. The orange corridor at the entrance is eye-catching
6. The unique mezzanine
7. Working staff
8. A corner of the lobby

7

8

KUUM Hotel Spa & Residences

Bodrum, Turkey

The KUUM Hotel Spa & Residences is an innovative concept for boutique lifestyle and resorts. The architecture for KUUM was inspired by the regional beauty, resources and historical legacy of southwestern Turkey and the Aegean Sea. Specifically, the Kuum Property is located in Bodrum, an international destination renowned for its wonderful climate, turquoise waters and cosmopolitan atmosphere.

The interior design of the lobby in the hotel is simple and natural. The platform beside the floor-to-ceiling window is set for guests to rest and enjoy the picturesque views outside the window where the sea and the continuous mountains act as a kind of decoration for the hotel.

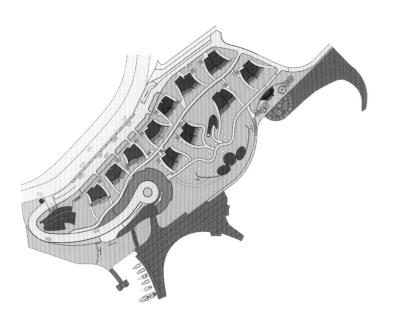

1. The design of the lobby is simple and natural
2. The use of floor-to-ceiling window allows the outside scenery to act as interior decoration

Lánchíd 19

Budapest, Hungary

Named after Budapest's famed "Chain Bridge" spanning the Danube and situated near both it and the Buda Royal Castle, the Lánchíd 19 has become a contemporary architectural landmark that attracts a new kind of cosmopolitan crowd. The Lánchíd 19 is a beacon of innovation while still paying homage to its historical settings – a perfect point of departure for discovering Budapest's wonders.

Principles of flowing space and light dominate the experience of this stylish urban get-away, from the glass atrium towering above the foyer to the rooms' and suites' open-plan design. The feeling of openness and transparency is enhanced by the clear views from the lounge to the restaurant to the intimate garden beyond.

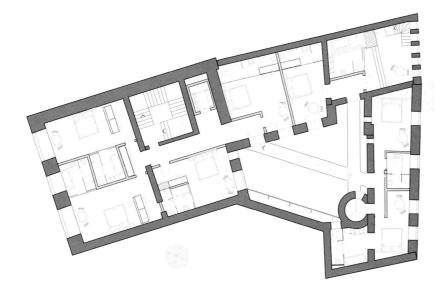

1. Sitting area in the lobby
2. The artistic lobby
3. "Floating" seats

Leon's Place Hotel

Rome, Italy

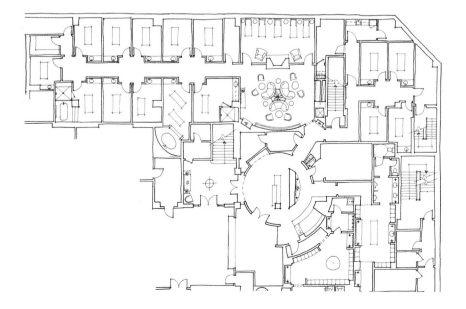

A short walk away from famous Roman sights like Via Veneto, Spanish Steps or Trevi Fountain, Leon's Place is the perfect home base from which to explore the Italian capital. Designed by Hotel philsophy's Creative Director Alvin Grassi.

Public areas are clean and contemporary as well, with noble retro decorations, offering a respite from the wealth of visual information outside. Speaking of respite, wellness is a priority at Leon's Place, whose Wellness Point features a sauna, steam bath and fitness centre staffed by specialists eager to pamper guests with facial treatments, body therapies and a range of massages. Both leisure and business travellers feel perfectly at home here, and might find themselves staying in to sample the international and Italian fine dining at Leon's Place Cocktail Bar & Restaurant, a culinary destination in itself.

1. Retro-style symmetry is applied to the lobby
2. The black swing chair enlivens the lobby
3. The reception is simple and clean
4. Interior furnishings
5. The interior design of the lobby is noble and orderly

Lux 11

Berlin, Germany

Just steps from the famous TV tower that soars over trendy Berlin-Mitte, Lux 11 is the perfect place for individualists who like just the right balance of pampering, style and autonomy.

Urban-lifestyle mavens who like having their fingers on the pulse of the action – more than a few celebrities have thrown parties here – prefer staying at Lux 11 for extended stays, as if they'd temporarily moved to Berlin's most vibrant neighbourhood and made it their very own. The lobby is quite lively. The designers boldly add some fashion styling and bright colours to the space, which thus becomes modern with a metropolitan air.

1. Reception
2. Sitting area

Marriott Marquis

Atlanta, USA

The $138 million renovation of this Atlanta landmark hotel respects the original Portman design while enhancing existing features and relocating all food and beverage outlets off the lobby bar, creating a hub of activity.

Phase II of the renovation was concluded in August 2008 and centres on the addition of the new Atrium Ballroom, the renovation of the existing Marquis Ballroom, the renovation of the main lobby and front desk, and the brand new fitness centre and spa. The main lobby received a completely new front desk, also curved to reflect the architecture of the atrium and designed in sections to allow employees to easily reach the guests.

1. Curved front desk
2. Lobby
3. Sitting area

Mauritzhof

Muenster, Germany

Hotel Mauritzhof is a member of Design Hotels TM. In the heart of Muenster, just a few steps from the historic town centre, lies the multifunctional Mauritzhof Hotel.

The Mauritzhof provides an intimate ambience with all the advantages of a top-class venue. The design of the hotel is functional down to the last detail without being cold. Pastel-coloured walls and the beechwood parquet floors help ensure a warm atmosphere. Bathed in natural light, Mauritzhof Hotel's revamped entrance serves as a transparent channel to a cool lobby and bar and creates an arena for conversation and interaction between guests and even locals.

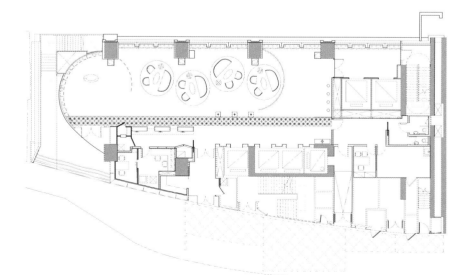

1. View of the entrance from inside the lobby
2. A corner of the lobby
3. Counter
4. Entrance
5. Reception

Mosaic Hotel

Delhi, India

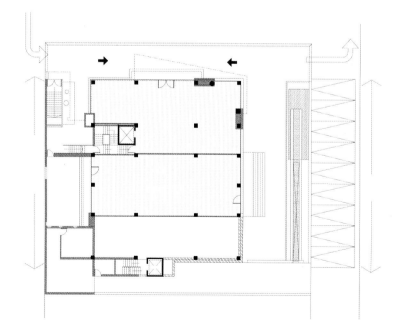

The design of the hotel completely corroborates the name. This is a hotel with a mosaic of experiences, a mosaic of colours, of textures, of lighting, of compositions, of forms, of spaces, each with a unique identity and yet integrated together holistically. The underlying concept was to redefine the way a hotel is perceived. The existing box-like structure was completely transformed by angular planes created to form a dynamic juxtaposition of form that delineates the structure now. Colour has been provided not in a static way by paint but in a dynamic way by colour-changing lighting that constantly transforms the lounge bar completely while being an important element in the lobby, in the form of projected glass modules from a marble clad wall. Textures imparted by natural-look materials play an important role throughout the interiors in the restaurant, the corridors and the rooms. Circular glass inserts in a 24'0" high wall with colour-changing LEDs keep changing the ambience in the lobby at regular intervals creating dynamism.

1. Lobby
2. Sitting area

Nanjing Central Hotel

Nanjing, China

The Nanjing Central Hotel is located in XinJieKou – the bustling centre for business and commerce in the city, with convenient transportation and a lively market.

The mastery of a unique style of architecture is paramount in allowing the building to stand out from other quality hotels in the surroundings. Instead of the simplistic, introverted mainstream style, the architects combined culture, aesthetics, market and operation. Backed by a European style and adorned with modern techniques, they seek to create a new charisma for the hotel without losing its grace and classical charm. The perfect fusion of architecture, function and decoration will bring a new view for the hotel.

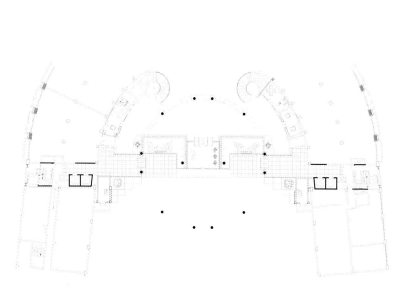

5

6

1. Sumptuous interior of the hotel
2. Landscape design for the atrium
3. The atrium landscape enlivens the hotel atmosphere
4. The carpet with peculiar patterns leads guests into the hotel
5. Lighting attracts guests to the reception
6. A corner of the lounge

Net Hotel

Padua, Italy

The hotel located in the tower from Level -2 to Level 9 represents a "business focused" hotel (based on the commercial market and business), in the category of "four stars plus", being an important landmark in the hospitality field not only for Padua city. The Convention Centre located at level -1 has been conceived in order to offer flexibility through the use of sliding walls that allow the zoning of the main room in two rooms.

In the common spaces, a series of sitting area are created for the hotel's guests to take a pleasant rest. In these areas, with modern design techniques, the designers successfully offer a simple but fashionable atmosphere. The aesthetic effect is achieved with the shapes of the areas themselves as well as the lighting design.

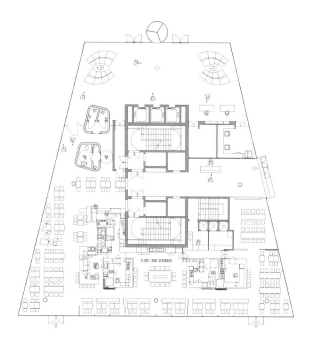

1. Reception
2. Sitting area
3. Lobby

Nhow Hotel

Milan, Italy

Nhow Hotel is located in a restructured General Electric plant, one of the biggest industrial buildings in the Via Tortona area, an industrial zone until the 1930s and now a neighbourhood of fashion and design.

Nhow Hotel is not just a hotel, but also an exhibition place, where structures and furnishings can change and combine to provide facilities for temporary events, fashion shows, art exhibitions held in collaboration with the Milan Triennale and a network of art galleries. The fulcrum of this fluid dynamism is the large lobby, which adapts to different activities, to the needs of the guests and the cultural dynamics of the city. All the common areas are spacious and mutable, while the eclectic, informal furnishings – a combination of anonymous design and one-offs by contemporary artists and designers – underline the character of the place.

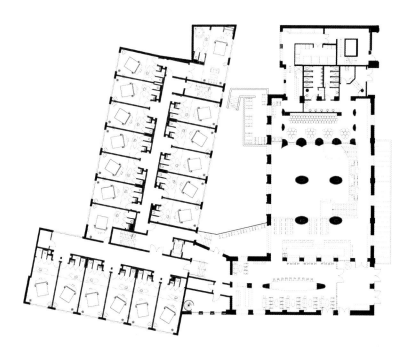

1. Artistic lobby reception
2. Specially-designed lighting
3. Specially-designed chair
4. Graffiti
5. The hotel looks like an exhibition hall

"NYLO" Hotel

Turkey

Dupoux Design aims to reshape the vision of the world we live in by changing the very space we inhabit. By projecting the past into the future, they hope to introduce a sense of familiarity to all that is yet unknown. That is why Dupoux Design strives to appeal to the subconscious by evoking all elements in design, which deal with all that is natural, unforced and soothing.

In the lobby in "NYLO" Hotel, the sofas seem embedded in the walls, which are wrapped with thick fabrics. The nearby partition is treated in a similar way. It seems that concrete is exposed on the walls and the ceiling. The neutral colour palette, as well as the compact yet comfortable layout of the areas, helps create an intimate and characteristic public space.

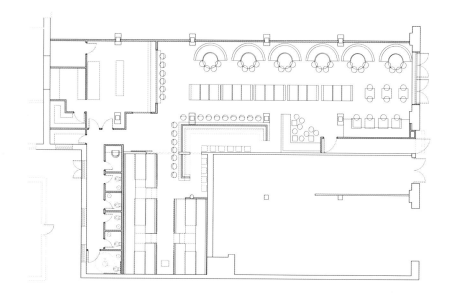

1. Game room
2. Library bar
3. Lobby

Palazzo Barbarigo sul Canal Grande

Venice, Italy

The hotel is located next to the Canal Grande, not far from Rialto Bridge and near the well-known Palazzo Pisani Moretta, and just few minutes walk from Piazzale Roma and the railway station. An exclusive haven of comfort recast by designer Alvin Grassi in feminine terms, a blend of past and present spiced with just a hint of the future, and a touch of the mystery that is Venice, the Hotel Palazzo Barbarigo sul Canal Grande is an Art Deco wonderland that amalgamates both the emotion and playfulness of the Venetian style.

The colour palette of the lobby is mainly black, with dark red and other neutral colours as decoration. The ingenious lighting creates a mysterious space instead of an otherwise dim and depressing environment.

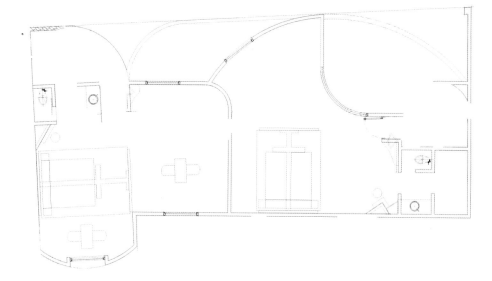

1. Lighting is a key in the interior lobby
2. The heavy books and the comfortable arm-chairs
resemble a noble study
3. Detail of the lounge
4. Reflection in the mirror

168 - 169

Quincy

Singapore

Quincy aims to fill the niche of providing sleek, ultra-contemporary digs for the consummate urbanite. Nestled in the heart of the busy city, its design direction is a boutique hotel whereby the theory of "form meets function", "style meets substance" is bridged. Quincy also aspires to provide exclusivity and a heightened sense of privacy away from the busy action located at a stone's throw. A weary traveller, a busy executive, or even a flustered family with kids, anyone can certainly find refuge upon finding this oasis of calm.

The interior design of the lobby is simple yet stylish. The round sofas evoke an intimate and comfortable feeling for guests. Lighting design follows the same style.

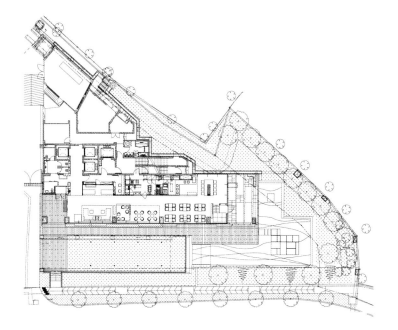

1. The cosy cobblestone-shaped chairs
2. The interior space is modern and quiet
3. The reception
4. The sparkling lighting of the reception at night
5. The corridor

Renaissance Boston Waterfront

Boston, USA

The Renaissance Waterfront serves as a sumptuous sanctuary for guests seeking to discover this exhilarating new public space. At the same time, this contemporary, dynamic hotel reflects all that is special about the waterfront, offering up a stunning and singular sense of place.

Centred on the adjacent park across the street, the transparent hotel entrance provides a dramatic view within – a view that after sunset, beckons visitors with welcoming, radiant light. Behind the front desk, an abstract art installation of fish bowls enhances check-in. These clear fish bowls contain resin in shades of watery blues and green poured at various angles, playfully mimicking the concept of sloshing water.

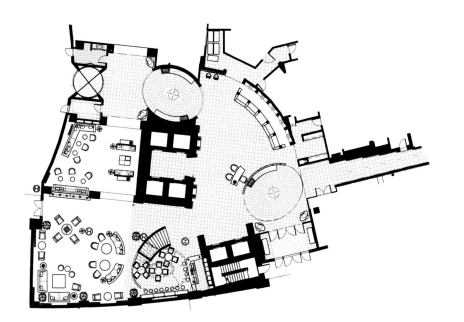

1. The ceiling height of the lobby highlights the sumptuous feeling
2. The circular gallary
3. The elegant and cosy lounge
4. The spiral stair

Renaissance Las Vegas

Las Vegas, Nevada, USA

The interior design of the hotel reflects the desire to create a unique hotel for Las Vegas, one that takes the best of Old Las Vegas – the sophisticated private clubs of the Rat Pack – and combines it with an environment designed to meet the needs of travellers, both business and personal.

The overall design is a timeless and subtle style as reflected in the choice of clean and simple furnishings and materials. The architectural detailing has its roots in mid-century modern design. Dry stacked stone and clean millwork take their cue from the Era, yet the design is clearly not imitating a 1950's style.

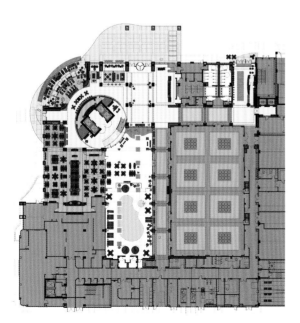

1. The lounge
2. A corner of the lobby

Risorgimento Resort

Lecce, Italy

The refurbishing of Risorgimento Hotel, in the historic centre of Lecce, has kept in a strong consideration the character of the original structure, with vaults in "leccese" stone and typical baroque decorations on the façade. The texture of the natural stone and the charm of the historic presences have been combined with contemporary furniture and dramatic lighting effects.

The lobby is designed both classical and modern at the same time. The lighting of the lobby is uniquely designed, offering different experiences during the day and at night. On both sides of the corridor, the designers adopted various furnishings to create the taste of the hotel.

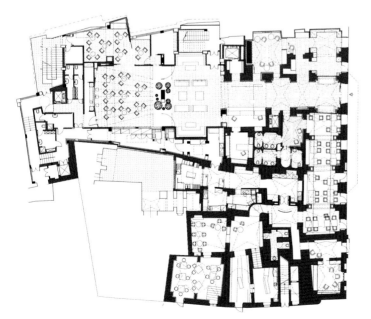

1. Reception in the lobby
2. View of the lobby from the entrance
3. Leisure area in the lobby

1

San Ranieri Hotel

Pisa, Italy

The feeling of overstepping the threshold of an illusory world is strong. Forthright surfaces and charming volumes interchange with penetrating chromatic lightnings that characterise the visual perimeter, underlining the intent to express contemporary times, beauty and renewed sense of content.

The hall is enriched by forthright white furnitures: it is inside this relaxing atmosphere that geometries find freedom of movements thanks to white veiled sheets that come down from the ceiling allowing the guest to always redefine the space, and to the sinuous continuity of the wall shaped with light white varnish plaster that divides technical function from the common ones and embodies the concept of "space box" playing with light and shadow.

1. On entering, you seem to step into a dream world
2. The all-white furnishings create a relaxing ambience
3. The colourful lighting contributes to a dynamic space

Shangri-La Hotel Tokyo

Tokyo, Japan

Completing the front desk is a gold-leaf coffer ceiling with gorgeous art work pattern. The front desk is made of a portoro stone slab finished off with beautiful bouquets of flowers at either side.

Dividing the front desk and lobby bar area, a focal decorative glass screen screens the lounge area, which adds contemporary elements to the space while lending a sense of intimacy and privacy to the area.

High windows accentuate the view which is framed with dramatic drapery. The rich palette in the hand-made area rug along with the silk, velvet and other rich fabrics gives the guest a rich tactile experience which can not be found in any other hotel.

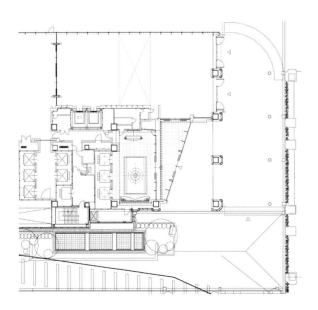

1. The reception in the lobby
2. The lounge
3. A corner of the lounge

Shima Kanko Hotel

Mie, Japan

HBA took into account the history of location and sensitivity to the environment when designing the interiors of the hotel. The element of water was a central design element and became the creative focus throughout the space. Modernity and refined elegance drive the esthetic design of this luxury suite hotel. Thousands of Mikimoto pearls were donated to the project and the designers gently added the shiny touches of elegance throughout the hotel.

The lobby is intimate in its boutique size and leads to a welcoming lobby lounge that boasts seating and a see-through fireplace. The back of the entry desk is flanked with hand-made stainless steel artwork in shape of waves.

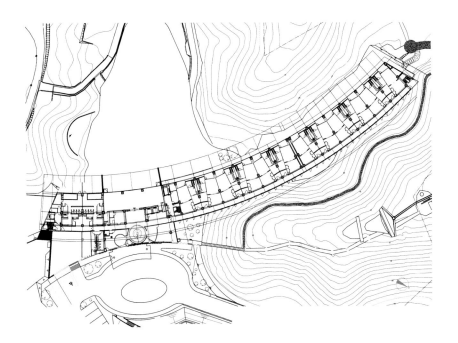

1. In the reception area, the element of water is incorporated in the wall, the floor and the decorative lamp
2. The delicate lamps
3. The cosy lounge
4. Guests can enjoy the picturesque views outside the window

Sofitel Lyon Bellecour

Lyon, France

This recent renovation has succeeded in bringing to the fore the prestigious character of a hotel that is a landmark in Lyon. The new sleek, yet welcoming and convivial interior is the product of the perfect complementary mix of traditional craft techniques and the designers' eclectic choice of the very finest of materials.

The patchwork of embroidery and prints decorates the walls of the lobby, in perfect contrast with the contemporary décor. The designers called on the services of artist Gille Cenazandotti for this part of the project. The aim is to give the hotel a true sense of identity and to avoid the merely decorative.

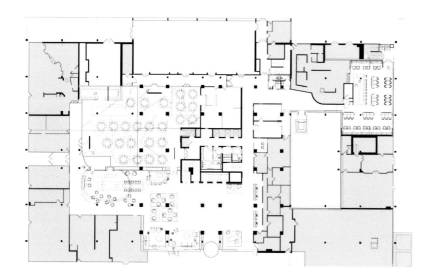

1. The delicate patterns on the carpet go well with the modern furnishings
2. The embroidery and the prints on the wall are eye-catching

Spa Hotel Bruendl

Linz, Austria

The three-storey lobby is a connecting link between the two structures which, however, simultaneously have the quality of serving as a multifunctional room and a tool which opens up into the restaurant, bar, therapy zone, rooms and spa.

The irregular-shaped lobby also acts as a circulation space. The railing of the surrounding corridors becomes a kind of decoration for the lobby when lit at night. The giant red pendant lamp, as well as the white glittering reception, is quite eye-catching. On the wall behind the reception, the free and simple graffiti corresponds with the central pendant lamp. Opposing the reception is a crimson wall which would lead guests to the inner part of the hotel.

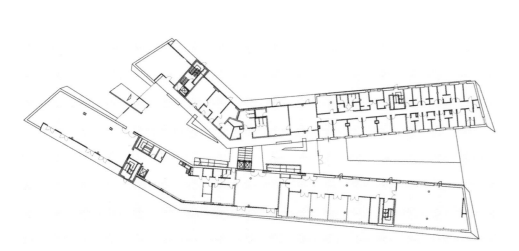

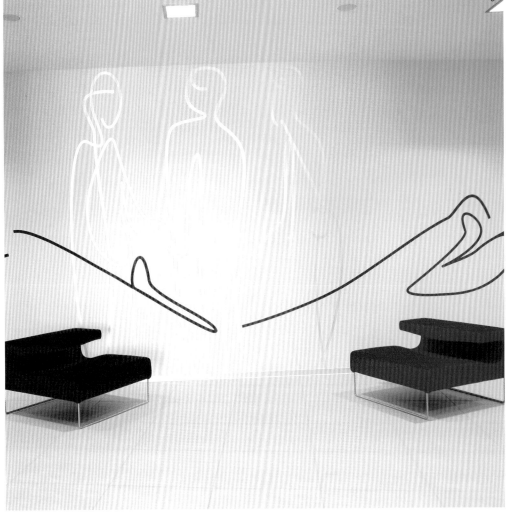

1. Overview of the lobby from the second-floor corridor
2. The open lobby
3. The red sofas and the graffiti on the wall

Stadia Suites

Mexico City, Mexico

The concept was to create a space that felt more like a private apartment than an unfamiliar hotel room.

On a tight budget, Farca furnished the project utilising pieces designed by his own company, combined with a few mid-century highlights, such as Bertoia Chairs in the breakfast room and lounge. A carved wood relief behind the reception desk is Stadia's signature design element, projecting warmth in its tone and sophistication in its modern form. Its modern geometries sensually affect the quality of light that engages visitors as they check in and out of the hotel.

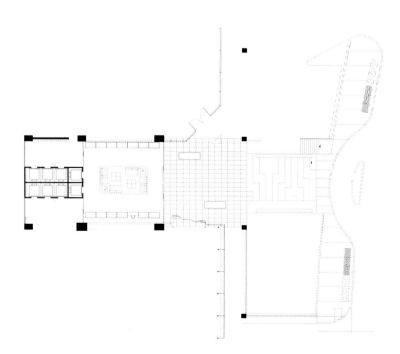

1. Entrance
2. Overview of the lobby
3. Sitting area
4. Sitting area
5. Sitting area

4

5

Talca Hotel & Casino

Talca, Chile

The hotel lobby is connected with the administrative offices by a triple-height space. Such a height should be well explored for the interior design of the lobby and this becomes the key for the designers. They divided the space by a triple-height "glass box", on which the black lines become a decorative element for the lobby while clearly defining the area. A similar pattern is adopted on the ceiling, resembling the pattern of brick walls. The giant orange pendant lamp makes the extremely high space feel comfortable. At the bottom of the "glass box", the black settees correspond with the black lines. Here guests would feel the grandeur of the space. The fervent colourful carpet draws attention downward.

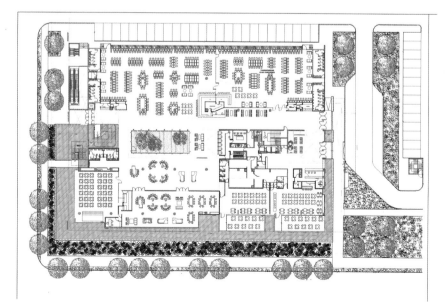

4

5

1. Black settees are set beside the "glass box"
2. The red squares decorate the wall and highlight the grandeur of the space
3. The giant orange pendant lamp
4. The brick-wall pattern is adopted on the ceiling
5. The eye-catching colourful carpet

"THE BUSAKORN WING"
Holiday Inn Resort

Phuket, Thailand

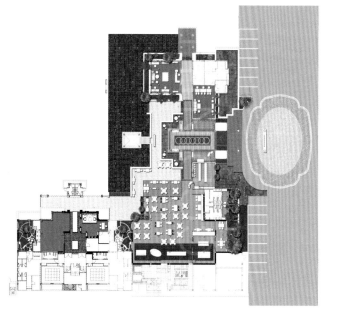

This is a superlative example of Chino Portuguese style where the oriental fuses with the Western. The design of this hotel shows the influence of Phuket inspired by the characteristics of the Phuket's building in town. The combination of the oriental and modernity balances the design in a temporal environment: illuminated column with the metal screen pattern, copper urn with cherry wood ceiling fan, and the handmade design lampshade providing a diffuse, glamour lighting completing a dramatic atmosphere.

Fans on the ceiling, decorative columns, and novel hanging lamps imbue the porch with character. The check-in room comprises a cosy lounge situated beneath a high ceiling. It is characterised by the combination of material and conformation.

1. Natural light and artificial light are used together to create a harmonious lighting environment
2. At the entrance, the ceiling, the pendant lamps, the columns and the pattern on the floor provide an imperial air

The Dominican

Brussels, Belgium

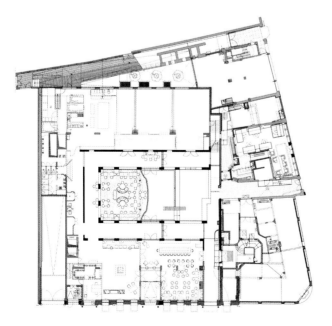

The Dominican is a new hotel that offers a strong sense of history mixed with forward-thinking, eclectic design in the European Union's capital city.

Guests enter the lofty, high-ceiling public spaces and their breath is taken away by the attention to detail and what the hotel has dubbed "dramatic intimacy". A stroll through the Monastery Corridor evokes an almost medieval feeling of elegance with original Belgian stone flooring. The Grand Lounge, considered the heart of the hotel, calls to mind the spirit of old European decadence in soaring windows and metalwork anf at the same time attracts a definitively style-conscious modern clientele with its cutting-edge design.

1. The lounge
2. White ottomans
3. A bit of blue enlivens the white-palette space
4. The entrance

The Europe Resort Killarney

Killarney, Ireland

The resort hotel and spa exudes contemporary, natural luxury as it overlooks Killarney's majestic Loch Lein. According to HBA's London Director, Inge Moore, "Hotel Europe represents a breakthrough in innovative luxury design in this part of Ireland. It sets a new kind of standard for hospitality – there's nothing like it in the region." The bespoke design vision and precision details should certainly galvanise the unique property within the upper-end market.

"Conversely," she continued, "the lobby, the restaurant, and the massive spa leverage unique patterns and vivid colours, tempered by cosy fireplaces and intimate spaces for conversation or relaxation. The whole project is very quirky and much more colourful than many of HBA's previous projects."

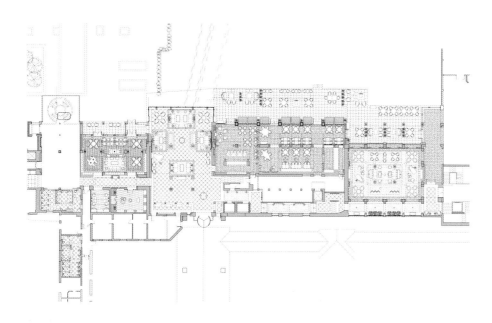

1. The coast scenery outside the window
2. The exquisite furnishings
3. The dark colour palette conveys luxury
4. The lounge immersed in sunshine
5. A comfortable armchair is set beside the fireplace
6. The lounge

The Gray

Milan, Italy

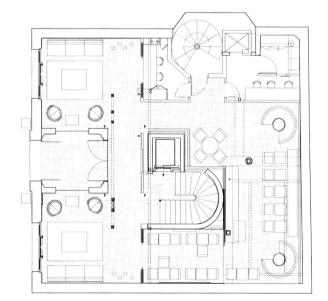

The Gray is ideally located right in the heart of Milan, a city that never sleeps. From its privileged position in Via San Raffaele, it is just round the corner from the Duomo and La Scala or even a short walk to the Galleria (Vittorio Emanuele). Designed with Milan's most exclusive fashionista set in mind, the simply-named Gray treads a careful line between elegance and opulence. Unashamedly elitist and purely residential, only the most established names are granted access to The Gray's private club-like atmosphere, housed in what were once residential buildings.

Guests are welcomed into a sumptuous lobby featuring a swinging red velvet divan and bathed in an ever-changing myriad of coloured light.

1. Red velvet divan
2. A corner of the lobby
3. Red velvet divan
4. The lobby with a peculiar taste
5. Red velvet divan

The Hazelton Hotel

Toronto, Canada

The five-star hotel imparts the warm intimacy of a manor home. Classic designs receive a modern update with inviting textures and superb craftsmanship.

Designed in the flavour of a large great room, the lobby space is defined by decorative metal screens which add artistic interest. Walls are covered in supple leather panels, while a custom cove ceiling features a sculptural scallop pattern. Dressed in a subdued palette, the lobby has a masculine flavour which sets the tone for the hotel and is interspersed with moments of glamour. Located off the lobby is a small jewel box of a reception area. Panelled in charcoal grey cowhide, the space has a refined sophistication. A sculptural bronze reception desk makes a luxe statement.

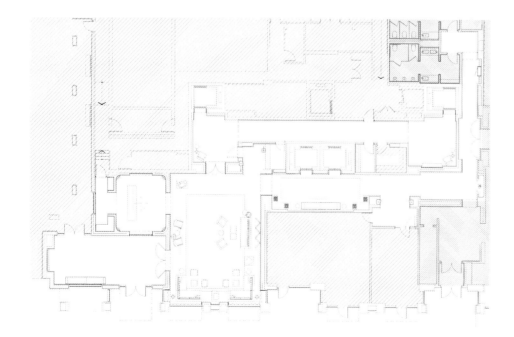

1. The combination of metal decoration and marble creates an unexpected effect
2. The noble style continues from the partitions to the furnishings
3. The lamp beside the couch and the little stools are the key points
4. Sculptural bronze reception desk

4

The New Majestic Hotel

Singapore

The project is to revamp a historical hotel on a street once known for its sex appeal. Inside, the juxtaposition of antique and modern, interior and exterior, pushes boundaries. An open-concept period-inspired lobby shows the imaginative possibilities of this marriage of old and new, or "heritage chic", as the hotel calls its particular design savvy.

DP Architects gave the lobby an intriguing transient feel. Sliding glass doors welcome guests into a large, high-ceiling space with walls, column supports, and floors in white terrazzo that emphasise spaciousness. The building's original ceiling was left stripped and raw with an uneven surface of concrete, wood and peeling plaster, and the whooshing antique Compton fans attached to it are new.

3

4

1. The spacious lobby
2. The white spiral staircase
3. The classical colour match of black, white and red
4. Unique furnishings

The Opposite House

Beijing, China

The architectural concept of the hotel was developed from the traditional planning of Chinese courtyard house that encapsulates private quarters with a central courtyard. All the spaces in the hotel evolved around the large central atrium. The seamless spatial sequence can be experienced through a series of light screens made with different materials throughout the public area to the guestrooms.

The design of the lobby is extremely artistic. The perfect colour palette and the dynamic effect of light and shadow are the most luxuriant decoration. In addition, pieces of artwork with a distinctive Chinese feature are placed. Here is a luxurious world of dream. The translucent interior partitions, on the one hand, are no harm to the spacious sense of the lobby, and on the other hand, diversify the space.

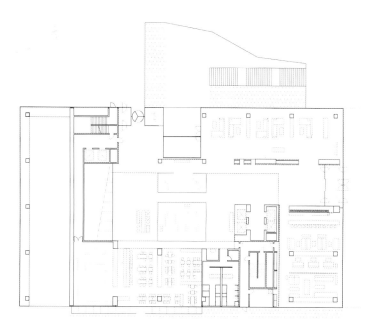

1. Distant view of the reception
2. Sitting area with soft sheers
3. Soft decoration on the ceiling
4. The dreamy light-and-shadow effect in the lobby

The Vine Hotel

Funchal, Madeira, Portugal

Arriving at the hotel, the great purple staircase and the metal mesh symbolise the summer rain, giving the guest the warm welcome.

In the lobby, the restaurant "Terra Lounge" represents the vineyards, and the garden with all the sofas are like big baskets of harvest and the purple cushions, the colour of the wine.

The floor finishing is covered with small round pebbles, representing the beaches of pebbles on the Island.

The designers chose the colour purple for the lobby interior, a colour that is usually difficult to handle, in order to create a different space. The colour is well explored with lighting, fully demonstrating its mystery and sensibility. The interior design is not complicated. Lighting and colour are the two key elements which are utilised to the full. The glaring furniture, the wash painting patterns on the wall, the cloud-like central sofa, and the tassels beside the staircase together create a dreamy space.

1. Lighting is an excellent interior decorative element
2. The interior design is simple yet romantic
3. The rounded fabric sofa in the atrium
4. The spiral stair is decorated with tassels and the lighting belts on the ceiling

The Wit Hotel

Chicago, USA

At the heart of the legendary Loop, the life of a great city – its grit, its glamour, its great and famous wind – inspires an exciting new hotel that lives up to its name, the Wit.

The Loop is about glitter as well as grit, and the light and sparkle of the surrounding theatre district resonate in a striking, six-metre lobby mural and in the refractions and reflections of a "sensitive" lobby wall. The reception desk is a play of light and dark, reflection and refraction. Thousands of individual mirrors, set at various angles, create a shimmering effect at the back wall while the front desk reflects the lobby seating beyond.

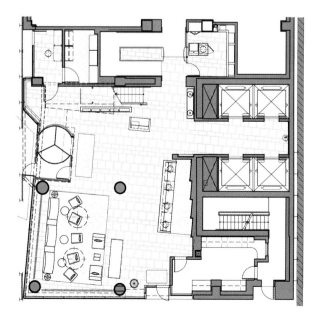

1. The lounge is suitable for reading and relaxing
2. Wall painting beside the stair
3. The reception desk
4. Aerial view of the lobby
5. The design of the details reflects the theme of wit

T Hotel

Cagliari, Italy

The T Hotel rises out of Cagliari's future cultural centre: the Parco della Musica, a verdant area with fountains and gardens, in which the hotel and the Teatro Lirico hold centre stage, will also contain an open amphitheatre, a contemporary art space and a theatrical stage design laboratory.

The higher structures penetrate space with their blue and green colouration, much like higher musical notes, while the lower structures fill the space with hues of red and orange, in rhythm with the lower musical notes. Depending on the wing they are located in, the rooms have four dominating colours: vital orange, dynamic red, relaxing green and serene lilac.

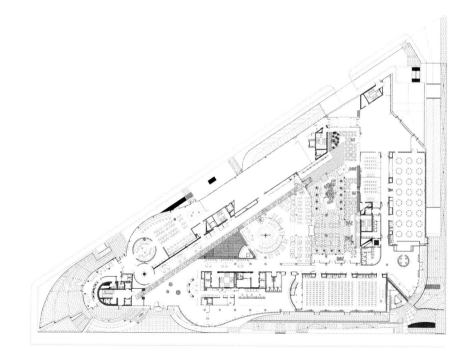

3

1. Reception
2. Night view of the outdoor recreation area
3. Cabinet
4. Sitting area
5. Curve wall

Uma Paro

Paro, Kingdom of Bhutan

Perched on a hill in one of the most untouched countries on earth, Uma Paro is a dramatic inland resort enveloped by snow-capped mountains, blue-pine forests and an ancient mountain culture. The resort was designed in collaboration with traditional Bhutanese artisans: indigenous detailing adorns interiors, walls are hand-painted by local artists, and the entire complex is arranged to resemble a traditional Bhutanese village speckled with orchards, lawns and flower gardens.

On the one hand, the designers used large amount of local wood and stone as decoration, bringing local natural resources inside. On the other hand, they adopted modern materials and design approaches, together with local decorative elements, creating a characteristic and stylish interior.

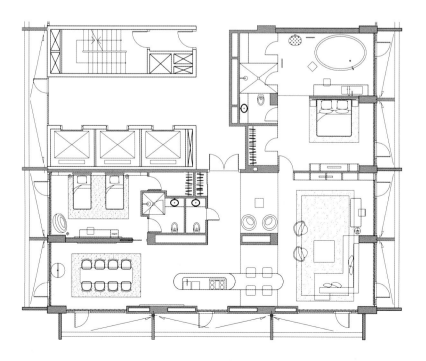

5

6

1. Delicate décor in the lounge
2. The materials of wood and stone convey the local flavour
3. The circulation area
4. A corner of the lounge, providing Internet services
5. The reception
6. A corner of the lounge

UNA Hotel

Bologna, Italy

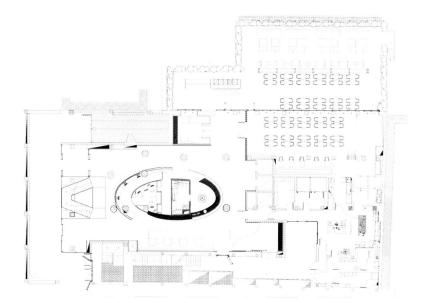

Like any other meeting and exchange venue, Bologna functions as a crossroads of habits, customs, languages and thus also of writings. It therefore seemed to designers to be consistent to adopt writing as the unifying and descriptive element of this new "place" dedicated to tourism. This is why certain languages/writings were chosen to denote the convergence of the various cultures. The other conceptual assumption that they found particularly interesting and synchronous with the theme of designing places, like the one in question, dedicated to movement is that of the relationship between writing and travel.

The lobby is quite modern. The designers chose black and silver – the colours reminiscent of modern technology – to match the simplicity style of the space.

1. The lobby features flowing lines
2. Dreamy effect

UnoaUno Hotel

Rimini, Italy

The interior space is simple and clean. The reception desk and the wall behind it are round-cornered in order to erase the hard edges. The giant black-and-white painting spread on the whole wall, adding some fashionable taste to the space. The unique patterns on the columns, ceiling and floor effectively enliven the space. The giant cylinder-shaped lamp hung on the ceiling offers an unexpected effect. Light beams are cast on the furniture, floor and frosted glass board. In such an environment, guests would feel as if they were in a fantastic space of the future.

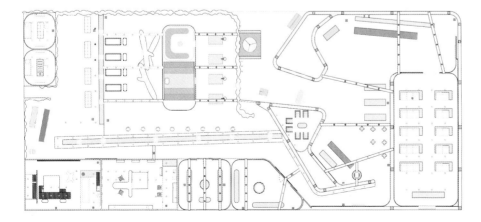

1. In the black-and-white space, the painting on the wall becomes the focal point
2. The orange reception desk is quite eye-catching
3. The giant pendant lamp hung on the ceiling

V8 Hotel

Stuttgart, Germany

Stuttgart and its surroundings are without doubt greatly influenced by the automotive industry. The Meilenwerk is a magnet for automotive clubs and a pearl for individualists who expect something more than just an exhibition.

The lobby is where a hotel leaves the first impression on its guests and visitors. In V8 Hotel, the comparatively small lobby is full of the prevailing driving culture. A car, as well as a motorcycle, is strikingly placed beside the reception. The logo on the reception and the poster on the wall highlight the same theme. The red sofa placed at the entrance symbolises the warm hospitality of the hotel, attracting visitors to come in and experience the unique feature of V8.

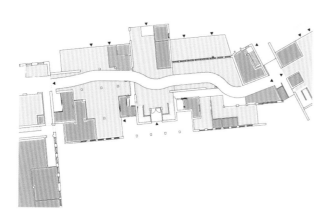

1. The entrance
2. View of the entrance from the hotel inside

Villa Florence Hotel

San Francisco, USA

Mixing modern furniture with classic architecture, SFA Design created a relaxing home away from home for anyone seeking a more personal escape in an expansive urban setting. Stepping onto the Dijon-mustard, gold and cream terrazzo flooring of the foyer and greeted by an old painted mural of Florence, the ambiance is one of an expensive, yet intimate Italian home. Whimsical rugs and eclectic accessories from various antique stores and odd shops further this sense of an isolated Italian dwelling, always with a hip nod to the chic influences of modern boutique design. Clean-lined reception pods feature custom living glass panels lit from above to illuminate encased silk, vintage Italian scarves.

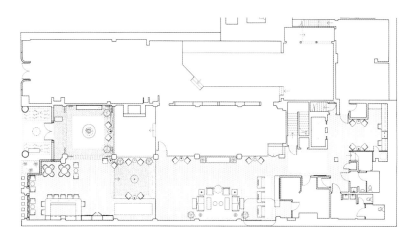

4

1. The spacious lobby
2. An escape in an expansive urban setting
3. The Italian luxury and comfort
4. The careful choices of table lamp, vase, and wall painting

Westin Hotels and Resorts

Hyderabad, India

The hotel is situated in the high-tech city in Hyderabad, an area that has gained the fame of "new Silicon Valley in India". The aim of the lobby design is to create a "sensational welcome" for guests. As you enter the lobby, the soft tones, soothing music and enchanting fragrance would lead you to a dreamy world. The designers intended to evoke your sensational experiences with the sober fragrance, elegant lighting, relaxing music and inviting greenery. The plants, including White Tea by Westin and innovative designs provided by the world-renowned floral designer Jane Packer, complete a fresh and cosy atmosphere that would erase travellers' fatigue immediately as they indulge themselves in the pleasures brought by the sensational experiences.

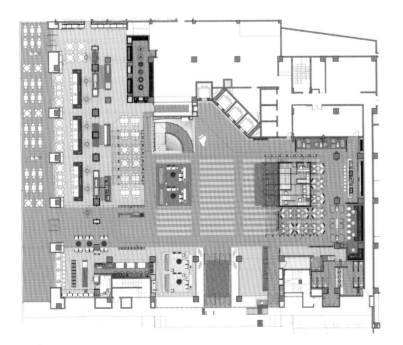

1. The decorations with the local feature are combined with modern furnishings
2. The atrium
3. The entrance
4. The bright lobby at night
5. The spiral staircase in the atrium

W Seoul Hotel

Seoul, Korea

In W Seoul Hotel, a striking lobby invites you to travel inside and creates in its visitors reaction and emotion. Its expressions are not minimalist but they are certainly modern, bringing back the feelings of warmth, of all that is casual, but comfortable in a modern way.

The designers challenged this grand-scaled lobby of being lost and boring, thus making it into a series of interesting focal points that unite in a consistent effort and that can be perceived from every corner and perspective. You may choose to slink into one of the egg-shaped chairs suspended from the ceiling and sip something cool, and then head upstairs where cabanas encircle the glowing first-floor lounge, offering a private view of the action below.

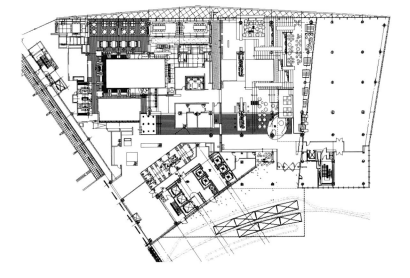

1. The mysterious purple lighting
2. The pendant lamps are eye-catching
3. The playful egg-shaped chairs
4. The interior is simple and clear
5. Lighting helps create an elegant air

Wynn Macau

Macau, China

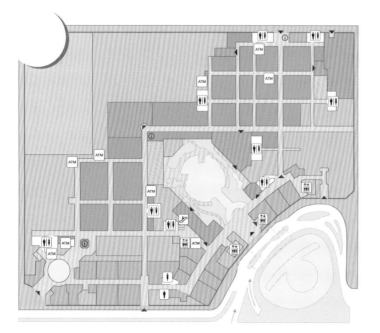

The retail esplanade at Wynn Macau houses exclusive and luxury shopping boutiques in approximately 46,000 square feet of exquisitely-designed retail space.

The fountain's performance results in lofty plumes of water and fire that dance to music and permeate the lush surroundings. The centrepiece of the entire atrium is an iconic Golden Tree of Prosperity that rises up from below and dazzles with its golden leaves and branches. The 21-metre-diameter gold cupola in the ceiling features twelve sculpted, dynamic animals from the Chinese zodiac. The 11-metre-diameter sparkling chandelier is composed of 21,000 crystals. Echoing the Chinese zodiac cupola is a dome of the western zodiac on the floor. The 10-metre-diameter copper dome, engraved with 18th-century astronomic charts, features twelve astrological signs.

1. The landscape outside the window matches the sumptuous interior decoration
2. Giant crystal lamp
3. Copper dome of the atrium

Yas Hotel

Abu Dhabi, UAE

The lobby lounge occupies a continuous bay adjacent to the reception and offers a range of seating areas, depending on the mood or the size of the group.

Laser-cut suede curtains enclose soft low seating. These curtains are a modern interpretation of the Arabian mashrabiya, affording discretion and privacy while allowing tantalising glimpses of flickering movement. The pattern is reminiscent of corals, sea urchins and anemones, and the light casts intricate, decorative shadows onto adjacent surfaces. The curtains also define zones within an otherwise free-flowing space. The main seating zone is defined by a chandelier reminiscent of a circling shoal of sardines.

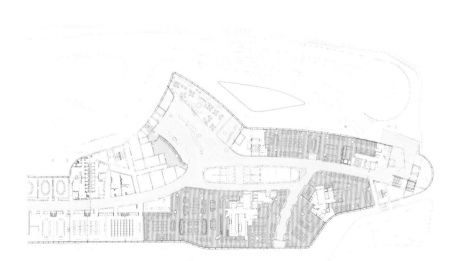

1. The lobby is a comfortable and casual space
2. A corner of the lobby

Index

Hotel Mod05
Designer: Andrea Aloisi & Enrica Mosciaro
Photographer: Ciro Frank & Schiappa

Hotel Modera
Designer: Corso Staicoff Inc.
Photographer: Jeremy Bittermann, David Phelps & Dan Tyrpak

Hotel Monaco Alexandria
Designer: Cheryl Rowley Design, Inc.
Photographer: Cheryl Rowley Design, Inc.

Hotel Murano
Designer: Corso Staicoff, Inc.
Photographe: John Clark & David Phelps

Hotel Palomar Arlington
Designer: Cheryl Rowley Design, Inc.
Photographer: Cheryl Rowley Design, Inc.

Hotel Palomar Dallas
Designer: Cheryl Rowley Design, Inc.
Photographer: Cheryl Rowley Design, Inc.

Hotel Palomar Los Angeles
Designer: Cheryl Rowley Design, Inc.
Photographer: Cheryl Rowley Design, Inc.

Hotel Palomar Washington
Designer: Cheryl Rowley Design, Inc.
Photographer: Cheryl Rowley Design, Inc.

Hotel Rho Fleramilano
Designer: Caberlon Caroppi Hotel & Design
Photographer: Lorenzo Nencioni

Hotel Ritter
Designer: JOI-Design

Hotel Villa & Resort Luisa
Designer: Alberto Apostoli Architecture & Design
Photographer: Davide Mombelli

Hotel Watt 13
Designer: Caberlon + Caroppi Hotel & Design

Ink 48
Designer: Rockwell Group
Photographer: David Phelps

InterContinental Hotel
Designer: Dileonardo International

I-Point Hotel
Designer: arc, Paolo Lamber, collaborator Pierpaolo Cenacchi
Photographer: Coopsette, Pierpaolo Cenacchi, Marina Chiesa, Mario Lamber

JinxiuJingya Hotel
Designer: Shanghai Infix Design
Photographer: Fang Jia

JW Marriott Hotel Beijing
Designer: HBA/Hirsch Bedner Associates
Photographer: HBA

Kempinski Pragelato Village & Spa Piedmont
Designer: THDP (The Hickson Design Partnership srl) / Nicholas Hickson & Manuela Mannino

KLAUS K
Designer: Stylt Trampoli
Photographer: Stylt Trampoli

Kruisheren Hotel
Designer: Henk Vos
Photographer: Design Hotels

KUUM Hotel Spa & Residences
Designer: Global Architectural Development
Photographer: Ali Bekman & Ozlem Avcioglu

Lánchíd 19
Designer: Péter Sugár, Lázló Benczúr/Dóra Fónagy (D24)
Photographer: Péte Sugur

Leon'S Place Hotel
Designer: Studio Jean-Pierre Rio and Alvin Grassi
Photographer: Studio Jean-Pierre Rio and Alvin Grassi

Lux 11
Designer: Guiliana Salmaso
Photographer: Silvestrin/Salmaso, London

Marriott Marquis
Designer: Thompson, Ventulett, Stainback & Associates
Photographer: Thompson, Ventulett, Stainback & Associates

Mauritzhof
Designer: Rainer M. Kresing
Photographer: Rainer M. Kresing

Mosaic Hotel
Designer: Sanjay Puri Architects Pvt. Ltd.
Photographer: Vinesh Gandhi

Nanjing Central Hotel
Designer: W To The Power Two Architects
Photographer: Gan Li

Net Hotel
Designer: Studio Marco Piva
Photographer: Studio Marco Piva

Nhow Hotel
Designer: Matteo Thun & Partners

"NYLO" Hotel
Designer: Dupoux Design

Palazzo Barbarigo sul Canal Grande
Designer: Alvin Grassi
Photographer: Alvin Grassi

Quincy
Designer: Ong & Ong Pte Ltd

Renaissance Boston Waterfront
Designer: Cheryl Rowley Design, Inc.
Photographer: Cheryl Rowley Design, Inc.

Renaissance Las Vegas
Designer: morrisonseifertmurphy
Photographer: morrisonseifertmurphy

Risorgimento Resort
Designer: scacchetti
Photographer: Marino Mannarini

San Ranieri Hotel
Designer: Simone Micheli
Photographer: Jurgen Eheim

Shangri-La Hotel Tokyo
Designer: HBA/Hirsch Bedner Associates
Photographer: HBA

Shima Kanko Hotel
Designer: HBA/Hirsch Bedner Associates
Photographer: Nacasa

Sofitel Lyon Bellecour
Designer: Studio Patrick Norguet
Photographer: Renaud Callebaut

Spa Hotel Bruendl
Designer: ISA STEIN Studio
Photographer: ISA STEIN

Stadia Suites
Designer: Invertierra Group/Jorge Dávila
Photographer: Paul Czitrom & Fernando Marroquín

Talca Hotel & Casino
Designer: Rafael Hevia García-Huidobro / Rodrigo Duque Motta
Photographer: Guy Wenborne, Rodrigo Duque Motta

"THE BUSAKORN WING" Holiday Inn Resort
Designer: Create Great Design Co., Ltd.

The Dominican
Designer: Lens Ass Architects & FG Stijl
Photographer: Lens Ass Architects & FG Stijl

The Europe Resort Killarney
Designer: HBA/Hirsch Bedner Associates
Photographer: HBA

The Gray
Designer: Guido Ciompi
Photographer: Guido Ciompi

The Hazelton Hotel
Designer: Yabu Pushelberg

The New Majestic Hotel
Designer: DP Architects Pte Ltd & Ministry of Design Pte Ltd / Colin Seah

The Opposite House
Designer: Kengo Kuma & Associates
Photographer: Katsuki Miyoshino

The Vine Hotel
Designer: Nini Andrade Silva

The Wit Hotel
Designer: Cheryl Rowley Design, Inc.
Photographer: InSite Architectural Photography

T Hotel
Designer: Studio Marco Piva
Photographer: Francesco Bittichesu

Uma Paro
Designer: Cheong Yew Kwan / Kathryn Kng
Photographer: Kathryn Kng

UNA Hotel
Designer: Studio Marco Piva
Photographer: Alberto Ferrero

UnoaUno Hotel
Designer: Simone Micheli
Photographer: simone micheli architectural hero s.r.l.

V8 Hotel
Designer: V8 Hotel in Meilenwerk
Photographer: Frank Hoppe

Villa Florence Hotel
Designer: SFA Design
Photographer: Ken Hayden

Westin Hotels and Resorts
Designer: CHADA
Photographer: Westin Hotels and Resorts

W Seoul Hotel
Designer: Studio GAIA, Inc.

Wynn Macau
Designer: Wynn Design & Development
Photographer: Wynn Design & Development

Yas Hotel
Designer: Jestico + Whiles
Photographer: Gerry O'leary